FLEMISH PAINTING

FLEMISH PAINTING

FROUKJE HOEKSTRA

PARK
LANE

Cover illustrations

- Rogier van der Weyden
  Portrait of Anthony of Burgundy, c. 1460 (detail)
  Brussels, Royal Museum for Fine Arts
- Joachim Patenier
  Charon Crosses the River Styx to the Underworld, c. 1522
  Madrid, The Prado

First published in Great Britain in 1994
by Grange Books PLC
The Grange, Grange Yard, London SE1 3AG

This edition produced in co-operation with Arcturus Publishing Ltd.

Translated from the Dutch by Tony Langham and Plym Peters

Coordination and production: VBI/Smeets, Weert
Filmset: Zspiegel grafische zetterij, Best, The Netherlands
Print: Royal Smeets Offset b.v., Weert, The Netherlands

© Royal Smeets Offset b.v., Weert, The Netherlands

ISBN 1 85627 697 X

FLEMISH PAINTING

The great age of painting in the Netherlands started at the end of the fourteenth century with the so-called Flemish Primitives, and lasted for more than three centuries until the end of the Golden Century. The whole area, which was divided towards the end of 1500 into the Northern and Southern Netherlands, produced an unbelievable amount of talent for that period of three hundred years, including some men of absolute genius such as Jan Van Eyck, Rogier van der Weyden, Hiernoymus Bosch, Pieter Bruegel, Rubens, Frans Hals, Rembrandt and Vermeer.

This edition contains a short survey of the development and influence of painting in the Southern Netherlands, particularly Flanders. This development runs from the International Gothic period at the end of 1300 to the Baroque era in the seventeenth century, of which Rubens is sometimes called the "father". Flemish art particularly had an international influence in the fifteenth century, especially on the surrounding countries, Germany and France, but during this period the influence even extended to Spain. At the end of the century the art of the Italian Renaissance was a great example for the whole of Europe, and this continued to be the case until the age of Rubens.

Jan van Eyck: Cardinal Nicolo Albergati, 1431
Silver burin, 21.2 x 18 cm
Dresden, Staatliche Kunstsammlungen

INTRODUCTION

From the beginning of Christianity until well into the Middle Ages, painting existed only in relation to church architecture. The vaulted ceilings, walls and pillars of churches were painted with religious scenes in which the figures bore no relation to reality. It was not the living, but saints who were depicted in these anonymous paintings, which for a long time followed the Byzantine tradition of painting strictly stylized figures against a decorative background without depth. (From the ninth century to the present day, the Byzantine tradition has remained virtually unchanged in the Russian art of icons.)

It is only in the thirteenth century that we come across a hesitant beginning of free or independent paintings; in other words, an art form that was not wholly in the service of the Church, and broke away from the strict traditions to make way for a more natural and free form of expression. The Italian painter, Giotto (c. 1267-1337), was one of the first to make his figures come alive, and he also used elements of landscape in the background. His work, and that of the generations of Italian painters who followed him, and who also started to paint worldly subjects, had a great influence on the development of the art of the European countries north of the Alps, and in France.

Surprisingly this development took place during a period in which Europe was ravaged by disasters, famine and war. The Hundred Years' War started in 1337; virtually the whole of Europe became embroiled in this war, which particularly affected France. Between 1347 and 1351, it is estimated that seventy-five million people died in Europe from the Black Death. Whole areas became virtually depopulated, and countries such as England and Italy lost a third of their population as a result of the plague. It was only in the Netherlands that the epidemic was limited to a small scale.

INTERNATIONAL GOTHIC

The royal residences in Paris and Prague were the most important centres of art and culture in the middle of the fourteenth century. There, the Gothic tradition, which was partly a continuation of the Byzantine culture, fell under the influence of Italy. In France, the Italian artists who worked at the papal court in Avignon played a significant role. Towards the end of the century a new style developed in western Europe, combining the Italian and Gothic traditions. This was the so-called International Gothic style, which was extremely influential.

The Flemish painters, who were already working at the courts of France (Paris) and Burgundy (Dijon) in the fourteenth century, were the artists who developed this style and heralded the golden age of Flemish painting. A large part of the work of the early Flemish "Primitives" - a term which became popular in the early nineteenth century, and which has obstinately survived, despite the fact it would be more accurate to refer to the paintings as early or old Netherlandish art - was actually lost during the wave of Iconoclasm in 1566, along with countless other religious works of art.

One of the most important representatives of the International Gothic style, the first Flemish painter whose name is known, is Melchior Broederlam; works can be attributed to him between 1381 and 1409. He lived in Ypres, and was court painter to the Count of Flanders and the Duke of Burgundy, Philip the Bold. The only works which have survived are the two side panels of an altarpiece which he painted for the Carthusian abbey of Champmol between 1392 and 1399. The composition of the holy figures is still in the Gothic tradition. The proportions are incorrect and there is no perspective, but the figures and garments are softly modelled under the Italian influence. One important element which is characteristic of the International Gothic style is the realism of the detail in the work: accurately represented foliage and a donkey that is true to life. Because of this careful attention to detail, the panel is reminiscent of a miniature, even though it is more than one and a half metres tall.

The art of miniatures had originated in the eighth century, and for centuries it was the only style of painting which allowed for any freedom. It started with "simply" decorated capital letters in religious manuscripts, but soon developed to become a sophisticated form of illustration in which the borders of the page were decorated with plants and animals copied from nature. In the course of time, there were more and more illustrations of saints in the manuscripts, and in the fourteenth century the illustrations rapidly became increasingly realistic. They even depicted scenes from daily life, and there were also landscapes.

The illumination of books was still the most important form of painting in northern Europe during the International Gothic period, although a start was made on the painting of panels. A good example of this illumination is the book of hours, *Les Très Riches Heures du Duc de Berry*, a masterwork made by the Limburg brothers (Pol, Jan and Herman, c. 1375/85-1416), who were born in Nijmegen. They were commissioned to do this work in 1413-1416 by the Duc de Berry, a brother of the King of France. The twelve pages of the calendar for the book of hours (a prayer book) are brilliantly detailed illustrations of the lives of peasants and noblemen in the twelve months of the year. *February* is not only the first winter landscape in the history of western art, but also the first work which depicts smoke and frozen breath. The details are brilliantly realistic, although the human figures are still stylized, idealized types. It is striking that the pages of the calendar do not contain any religious references - this means they are amongst the earliest examples of secular painting in northern Europe.

A NEW STYLE

In the fifteenth century the prosperous region of Flanders, with its wealthiest cities, Bruges, Ghent and Ypres, which still formed part of the Burgundian empire, developed to become the most important centre of European art after Italy. In both countries there was a revolution in painting, and the International Gothic style made way for attempts to represent the real world as it was perceived. Renaissance painting originated in Florence, and its rules were systematically developed to depict three-dimensional reality, resulting in the rules of perspective. Flemish artists discovered linear perspective as they worked, and experimented with blurred backgrounds to create an illusion of depth. However, the most important contribution of the Flemish painters to European art was the development of panel painting.

The first new impulses which changed the traditional imagery came from Robert Campin (c. 1375-1444), who was also known as the Master of Flémalle. However, some art historians doubt that Campin and the Master of Flémalle were the same person. This master painter from Tournai still worked in the International Gothic tradition, but added some new dimensions. His work had a greater plastic quality, and the realism of the details, attention to faces, and effective depth in the composition are characteristic of Campin, to whom Rogier van der Weyden was apprenticed in 1427.

Campin was one of the first to work in oils, but Jan van Eyck, who was for a long time viewed as the "inventor" of painting in oils, perfected this new technique and developed a completely new style. Jan van Eyck (c. 1390-1441), the first painter to sign his work, was the court painter of the Count of Holland and of Philip the Good, the Duke of Burgundy, for whom he also performed diplomatic missions. In 1430, he settled in Bruges, where he had an artist's studio which was to become the base for the School of Bruges. Van Eyck's technique in painting with oils is exceptional. His paint was so transparent that his works have a unique, almost luminous sheen. However, he certainly does not owe his fame only to this technique. He was faithful to nature, his figures were true to life, and his representation of space and his portraits made him one of the greatest painters of his time. His greatest work was the altarpiece, *Adoration of the Lamb*, for the Cathedral in Ghent, which he painted between 1425 and 1432. (His older brother, Hubert, started on this work, but died in 1426.) The naturalistic figures of Adam and Eve which are almost tangible, are particularly striking. In *The Madonna of Chancellor Nicolaes Rolin* (1435), Van Eyck revealed himself to be a master in the representation of space. The landscape in the background recedes in blurred greys, a so-called atmospheric perspective which is extremely effective. The celestial and earthly elements are side by side in this beautifully detailed painting - the precisely drawn Chancellor Rolin is seated opposite the idealized figure of Mary. Van Eyck probably produced his greatest work as a portraitist. The masterful *Man in the Red Turban* (1433), which is probably a self-portrait, reveals rare powers of observation and is, at the same time, an example of the magnificent way in which Van Eyck used light and dark, which remained unsurpassed for two centuries. The light also lends a special character to Van Eyck's greatest and most innovative portrait, *Giovanni Arnolfini and his Bride* (1434). The couple are shown standing in their room, with the light falling on them. The realistic quality is given an extra dimension by the mirror in the background, which reveals the presence of the painter and a witness.

THE SCHOOL OF BRUGES

Rogier van der Weyden (1399-1464), who was born in Tournai, was even more important for the development of Flemish painting. This apprentice of Campin's, who became the official painter to the city of Brussels, combined the new Flemish style of Campin and Van Eyck with the emotional drama of the Gothic style. Unlike Van Eyck, he devoted more attention to the general effect than to detail in his sophisticated and aristocratic portraits. In his work all the attention is focused on the foreground, and he was to be the greatest influence on northern European art until about 1500.

Jan van Eyck and Rogier van der Weyden were never surpassed by their immediate and by no means unimportant successors. These included Van der Weyden's presumed apprentice, the great portraitist from Germany, Hans Memling (c. 1433-1494), who was a master of subdued religious scenes, Petrus Christus (1415/20-1472), the painter of man in the landscape, Dirk Bouts (c. 1415-1475), and the melancholy and mystical Hugo van der Goes (1440-1482), who had a great influence on Italian painters. The last painters of the School of Bruges are the Master of the Legend of St. Lucia, who worked between 1483 and 1501, and who went back to the gothic ideals, and Gerard David (c. 1460-1523), who came from Holland. He was one of Memling's apprentices, and produced some strong and austere works. The Flemish-Spanish painter, Juan de Flandes (attributed to the years 1496-1519), has a special place in Flemish art. From 1496, he was court painter in Spain, and was responsible for the Dutch influence in Spanish art. Throughout the period of the School of Bruges, Flemish art was highly esteemed throughout Europe, both by painters and by artists. The painters were admired for their technique, and the painstakingly detailed landscapes in the background. In the sixteenth century this skill was valued so highly by Italian artists, that many Flemish painters worked in Italian studios for shorter or longer periods.

THE SIXTEENTH CENTURY

At the beginning of the sixteenth century, Antwerp became the most important city in Flanders. The river Zwin silted up, and the once powerful port of Bruges was cut off from the sea. During the same period, the Westerscheldt became much wider as a result of flooding by storms, and even sea-going vessels could reach the city. The new port quickly flourished, and the open climate of the city soon attracted artists as well. Thus when Bruges silted up, Antwerp succeeded it both from the cultural and economic point of view. The liberal atmosphere had an inspirational effect, and a new genre of painting, the landscape, which had up to then played a subordinate role, developed in the first decade of the sixteenth century.

Joachim Patenier (c. 1485-1524) was a key figure in this development. His paintings still contained figures, but they were completely integrated into the landscape, which was an entirely new departure. He created depth by modulating the colours from warm (green) to cold (greyish blue). This was an atmospheric perspective which Jan van Eyck had also used in his work almost a hundred years earlier. This effect of depth was accentuated even more strongly in the paintings of Herri met de Bles (c. 1500-1550/60), who was probably a nephew and apprentice of Patenier. His landscapes seem to gradually disappear in a soft mist towards the horizon, a sophisticated effect that seems quite natural.

The most important Antwerp master of the first half of the sixteenth century was Quentin Massys, in whose work man is the central element. He belonged to the circle of the Antwerp humanist Petrus Aegidius, and Erasmus, and was certainly influenced by their ideas. Massys represented his figures in an unusually penetrating and human way for that time. The large altarpieces had an extremely well-balanced composition, and a subtle use of colour expressed a sensitive view of the humanity of the holy figure. It is not known whether Massys travelled to Italy to study the art there, as was fashionable even in his time, but his work, which is based on the Flemish tradition, also revealed Italian influences (particularly those of Leonardo da Vinci).

Up to the beginning of the sixteenth century, Italian art only influenced a few painters in the Netherlands. But almost a hundred years after the Renaissance, which was based on the classical quest for beauty and harmony, had emerged in Italy, these ideas also appeared in the Southern Netherlands. They were influenced by Humanism, the main philosophy of the Renaissance, which was based on classical values (the dignity and rights of man and scientific thinking). The most important philosopher of this movement was the Dutchman, Erasmus.

The way in which the great Italian Renaissance artists (including such geniuses as Leonardo da Vinci and Michelangelo) interpreted and changed classical imagery, engendered great admiration and was widely followed. It became almost compulsory for a young painter to make the long journey to Italy, primarily to Rome, to study the classical and contemporary works in situ. A large group of leading Flemish artists incorporated the classical imagery so fully in their work in the first half of the sixteenth century that they were named "Romanists". One of the first important Romanists was Jan Gossaert, known as Mabuse (c. 1478-1532). He travelled to Italy in 1508 with his patron, Philip of Burgundy. Gossaert, who was initially a typical representative of the Flemish style, was completely enchanted by classical art, and started to work wholly from the example of his ideals. From this time, painting mythological scenes and nudes as the main subject also became popular in the Netherlands.

THE FLEMISH TRADITION

Not all Flemish painters were influenced by Italy, and in the first half of the sixteenth century two main movements arose in the Southern Netherlands: the movement which continued the Flemish traditions, and the movement which followed the Italian style (which not only included out-and-out Romanists). The latter movement gained the upper hand in the second half of the century, and pure Romanists such as Abraham Janssens (c. 1575-1632) continued to work up to the seventeenth century.

Amongst the painters who worked in the Flemish tradition there are a number who had a particular preference for scenes from daily life, a subject which had up to that time been used mainly as the "background" in miniatures. The greatest Flemish painter of this genre is Pieter Bruegel, whose name is inseparably associated with scenes of village life. However, he had a less famous predecessor, Jan Sanders van Hemessen (c. 1500-after 1575), who painted remarkable scenes from ordinary life in a strongly visual, realistic style which tended towards caricature. One of his well-known works is *The Surgeon* (c. 1555), a scene depicting the practices of "quacks", which was probably intended as a moralizing work, in view of the fifteenth century dress of the figures in the painting, which shows that the scene does not refer directly to contemporary life.

Moralizing scenes, which were popular at that time, are also common in the work of the most famous sixteenth century Flemish painter, Pieter Bruegel, who was probably born near Breda between 1520 and 1530, and died in Brussels in 1569. Bruegel was enroled in Antwerp as a freemaster in 1551. He travelled to Italy, but the only hints of this journey are to be found in his last works. It was only the landscapes which he encountered on the journey that constantly recurred in his paintings. The Roman Colosseum undoubtedly served as an example for the *Tower of Babel*, dating from about 1563, a magnificent panel in which Bruegel combined the skills of Flemish landscape painting with a tremendous, overpowering architectural structure. Bruegel was sometimes called the "new Hieronymous Bosch" by his contemporaries, and he certainly owed his early fame to prints commissioned by the famous publisher of prints, "In de Vier Winden", in the style of his illustrious predecessor. But he soon started working in his own style, and prints of series of his landscapes were published. Moreover, the trade in prints was a flourishing business from the time that the technique of copper engraving had been invented, as this allowed for the reproduction of works on a large scale. Original prints and copies of famous works were sold in their thousands so that an increasingly broad public became familiar with famous works of art. Bruegel owes his title "Peasant Bruegel" to a few works which have become world famous and which he painted towards the end of his life. However, these only constitute a small proportion of his impressive oeuvre which includes exceptional landscapes such as *Return of the Hunters* (1565), as well as symbolic works about the folly of the world, for example, *The Proverbs* (1559), biblical scenes and fantastic genre paintings in the style of Hieronymus Bosch.

Bruegel's work was extremely popular in his own time but he did not have any followers, because the Italian style had become dominant in the Southern Netherlands. Only his son, Pieter Bruegel the Younger, followed in the footsteps of his father, simply imitating his work.

THE LANDSCAPE

The love of detail which is so characteristic of Flemish (and Dutch) painting is reflected in the work of Bruegel's youngest son, Jan Brueghel (1568-1625). He became very famous for his elegant landscapes and floral arrangements. His landscapes were "distant views" which were characteristic of the sixteenth century style in the Southern Netherlands. These imaginary landscapes were composed in different levels, merging into each other without any linear perspective, and with a wealth of divergent themes. Towards the end of the century his vision of the landscape changed, and the foreground became the main element instead of serving mainly to create a sense of depth. Woods were first used as an independent subject, and mighty trees dominate the paintings of Gillis Van Coninxloo (1544-1607), a painter who fled the Catholic city of Antwerp in 1585 because of his religious beliefs, and arrived in Amsterdam in 1595. His view of the landscape was further developed by Gillis Claesz. d'Hondecoeter (c. 1575-1638), an Antwerp follower of the Reformation who also fled to Amsterdam.

On the whole the Flemish landscapes of the sixteenth century were landscapes in which various elements were combined to produce an ideal. One painter who fully exercised his imagination in this way was Roelant Savery (1576-1639). His imaginary landscapes were full of atmosphere and had an almost romantic quality. They were populated with all sorts of animals living peacefully side by side. These landscapes are almost diametrically opposed to the realism of Dutch landscapes which also emerged in this period.

RUBENS

The greatest and most influential painter, Peter Paul Rubens, who is known as the father of Baroque, was born in 1577 in the former German principality of Nassau, and died in Antwerp in 1640. The life of this painter and diplomat is closely linked to a decisive period in the history of the Netherlands. It was a time of great religious and political conflict, which had resulted in the Eighty Years' War in 1568. Tens of thousands of people in Flanders who had protestant sympathies fled from their country which was ruled by Spain, because they feared the Inquisition. These also included Rubens' parents, who fled to Germany where his father had a relationship with Anna of Saxony, the second wife of William of Orange. When this relationship was discovered he just managed to escape a death sentence, and was banished. After the death of Rubens' father the family returned to Antwerp in 1589. The city had been destroyed by the Spanish Fury. Very little was left of the most powerful port in Europe following the looting and the lengthy siege by the Dutch, who totally paralysed the port with a blockade. After the fall of the city in 1585 it slowly started to recover with the support of the Spanish governess, Isabella, while the war between the Northern and Southern Netherlands continued. Rubens later became court painter to Isabella, and as a diplomat in her employ he played a role in the endless peace negotiations with William of Orange. In his diplomatic capacity he also visited the great courts of Europe, where he was also valued as a painter and received many large commissions.

Following an apprenticeship with three masters, including Otto van Veen, the young painter left for Italy in 1600. He stayed there for eight years as the court painter to the Duke of Mantua, Vincenzo I Gonzaga. The Duke commissioned him to go to the Court of Spain for some time, combining diplomacy with painting. His first major commission in Italy was the triptych for the Santa Croce in Rome, which immediately brought him great fame. His most important works from this period are altarpieces and portraits commissioned by the Duke. However, for his development the most important aspect of his stay was the study of the classical and Renaissance masters. The Twelve Years' Truce was signed in 1609, shortly after Rubens' return to Antwerp for good. This heralded a period of recovery for the city and resulted in a flood of work for the painters of Antwerp. This was because the Spanish government wished to restore the churches destroyed and plundered by the looting Spanish troops during the wave of Iconoclasm (1566).

In 1608, Rubens was appointed painter to the city of Antwerp and court painter to the Archduke and Archduchess Albrecht and Isabella. A year later he married Isabella Brant, who died in 1626. In 1630 he was remarried, this time to Hélène Fourment. The painter established a large studio and soon received great commissions including the monumental triptych, "The Raising of the Cross", dating from 1610. In this work he achieved a synthesis of everything he had learned in Italy: the broad composition of Tintoretto, the plastic representation of figures in the style of Michelangelo, the warm Venetian colours. To these elements he added a new dramatic, emotive quality. The forceful diagonal line in the composition is surrounded by writhing, contorted bodies. This dynamic composition, which is also used in his countless mythological scenes, is typical of Rubens' style which entered the history of art as the Baroque style.

This unbelievably productive artist had a great influence on other painters with whom he often collaborated, such as for example Jan Brueghel and Anthony van Dyck (1599-1641). Rubens not only produced many works - about twelve hundred paintings are attributed to him - but also produced an enormous variety. The most important themes and subjects in the oeuvre of this genius include religious, allegorical and mythological scenes, portraits, hunting scenes and landscapes. He had a lasting influence on the art of the generations which followed him.

RUBENS' CONTEMPORARIES

Virtually all the Flemish painters from the first half of the seventeenth century can be related to Rubens in some way. The majority of these artists were completely overshadowed by the great master, often quite unjustifiably. Only a few have gone down in the history of art as important masters. This certainly applies to Anthony van Dyck, who is sometimes described as an apprentice of Rubens, though in reality he became a friend of Rubens when he was already a young master painter, and worked with him between 1617 and 1621. Van Dyck died at a young age but his career was comparable to that of Rubens. In 1630 he became the court painter to the Governess Isabella, and in 1632 he left for England where he became court painter to Charles I. Van Dyck loved travelling and had an extravagant lifestyle, and he was a masterful portraitist who depicted the aristocracy in sophisticated, elegant portraits, subtly revealing the character of his subjects. In Rubens' studio Van Dyck probably did not paint any special subjects, unlike Jan Brueghel, who was specially asked to paint garlands of flowers, as in the *Madonna in a Garland of Flowers* (c. 1616-1618), and background landscapes and animals. Another friend of Rubens and specialist in the studio was Frans Snijders (1579-1657), who was an excellent painter of still lifes and animals.

In some cases the relation with Rubens was less direct, as in the case of David Teniers the Younger (1610-1690). In his own time, Teniers was an exceptionally successful landscape, genre and portrait painter, with an oeuvre of about two thousand works. One of his paintings, which is a characteristic example of his work, is *The Art Collection of Archduke Leopold-Willem in Brussels* (1651), which shows the painter standing next to his patron surrounded by a gigantic collection of paintings. This work gives a good impression of the sort of collection owned by a nobleman at that time. It is interesting to note that these paintings often show works which have been lost in the course of time, and in this way form an important source of information for art historians. The influence of Rubens can be discerned in Teniers' later work. He married the daughter of Rubens' friend, Jan Breughel, and in this way entered the circle of acquaintances of the great master.

Jacob I Jordaens (1593-1678) married the daughter of Adam van Noort, one of Rubens' teachers. He was esteemed so highly that he received all the biggest commissions after the death of Rubens in 1640, and of Anthony van Dyck in 1641. Together with the father-in-law of Snijders, Cornelis de Vos (1584-1651), and a host of other Flemish painters, this celebrated painter produced the festive decorations designed by Rubens for the official entry of the Cardinal-Infant Archduke Ferdinand into Antwerp in 1635. These two artists also worked on the paintings for the hunting lodge of the King of Spain. Towards the end of his life Rubens made a large series of panels for the hunting lodge depicting mythological scenes. Jordaens was famous as a genre painter and was particularly popular for his Baroque and vivid scenes from the lives of the people of Flanders.

The life of the people was also the central subject of the work of Adriaen Brouwer (c. 1606-1638), who died at a young age. This painter was born near Leiden, worked in the studio of Frans Hals for a few years and then moved to Antwerp. He painted mainly scenes in inns and gaming halls, in a particularly lively, almost impressionist style. His work was also popular with painters, and both Rubens and Rembrandt owned some of his works.

STILL LIFES

One genre which developed in the seventeenth century and was exceptionally popular until the start of the eighteenth century was the still life. During this period several hundred Flemish and Dutch painters specialized in this genre, which produced countless masterworks of technical perfection and virtuosity. The painstaking and careful representation of "still" objects was striking in the work of the first master of painting in oils, Jan van Eyck, who had lived two centuries earlier. Representing plants and flowers in a way which was true to nature had started even earlier, in illuminated manuscripts. However, it is remarkable that these objects and flowers, which had played an incidental role for centuries, developed to become a popular subject in their own right. The development of this genre in the northern Netherlands could be explained by the fact that it was the perfect genre to suit the Calvinist taste for sober images. There was no more enthusiasm for the Baroque exuberance of the Flemish painters with their vehement, violent and dramatic mythological and biblical genre works. Therefore it is quite understandable that landscapes, architecture and portraits became the favourite subjects of seventeenth century painting, and the still life was soon added as another popular genre. However, it is curious that the still life was developed by Antwerp artists as an independent genre at the end of the sixteenth century - i.e., in the Catholic Southern Netherlands - and spread from there to the north.

The Flemish artists played an important role in the emergence of this genre in the Northern Netherlands. For example, Ambrosius II Bosschaert (1573-1621) fled from Antwerp to Middelburg because of his religious beliefs before reaching the age of twenty, and for the rest of his life he worked in Holland where he had a great deal of influence. The floral paintings of this early master of this genre also have a symbolic meaning, which applies for all still lifes, even though the symbols are often hidden from contemporary eyes. Some of the common symbolic elements include flies and empty shells which are a reminder of the transient beauty of earthly existence. A carnation symbolizes the humanity of Christ and probably every flower in the large bouquets had a special significance apart from its aesthetic one. The still lifes of flowers by Daniel Seghers (1590-1661), an apprentice of Jan Brueghel, should not be seen merely as botanical studies either. In fact, one of the curious features in Seghers' work is that in his still lifes he often incorporated portraits or religious scenes, which almost served as a background.

Only eight works have survived of the last of the early Flemish still life painters, Ossias Beert (1570-1624?). These were the precursors of a type of ornamental still life that became very popular in Holland, later known by the term *Breakfasts*. *Oysters and glasses* is a typical example of his work, and of the many later works which were variations on this theme. It depicts rich glassware, oysters, nuts and a bread-roll with the inevitable fly, the symbol of transience. With the still life painters, the golden age of Flemish and old Netherlandish painting came to an end. They were the last masters in an illustrious series of painters who set the tone for the art of northern Europe for two centuries without interruption. However, the heyday of painting in the Netherlands was not yet over; the golden century had started, introducing the era of the Dutch masters.

Melchior Broederlam
demonstrable between
1381 and 1409
The Presentation in the Temple
(detail) 1399
Right-hand panel of an altar
triptych in the Carthusian
monastery at Champmol
Dijon, Musée des Beaux-Arts

Broederlam is the first Flemish panel painter whose name we know. He did not respect perspective and proportions in this painting, which reveals a careful and realistic representation of the faces.

The Limburg Brothers, c. 1375/85-1416
The Month February, from the book of hours, "Les Très Riches Heures de Duc de Berry", 1413-16
Parchment, 22 x 13.5 cm, Chantilly, Musée Condé

Jan van Eyck, c. 1390-1441
The Madonna with Chancellor Nicholaes Rolin, c. 1435
Panel, 66 x 62 cm
Paris, The Louvre

The detail of the landscape in the background, the flowerbeds and the different materials is quite astonishing. It is a curious fact that during this period babies were apparently not studied very carefully. The baby Jesus looks like a miniature adult.

Jan van Eyck, c. 1390-1441
Man with a Red Turban, 1433
Panel, 25.7 x 19 cm
London, National Gallery

A brilliant small portrait, in which the striking turban draws all the attention to the finely represented face of a man, which could be a self portrait.

Jan van Eyck, c. 1390-1441
Giovanni Arnolfini and his Bride Giovanna Cenami, 1434
Panel, 81.8 x 59.7 cm
London, National Gallery

A brilliant detail in this painting is the mirror in the background, which shows the couple from the back, as well as two people in the space in front of them, outside the main picture. These are probably witnesses of the wedding, and one of them is Jan van Eyck himself. The panel contains countless symbols of marriage, such as the bridal candle and the little dog, which represents fidelity.

Petrus Christus, 1415/20-1472/73
St. Eligius, as a goldsmith, hands
the wedding couple a ring
1499, panel, 99 x 85 cm,
New York, Metropolitan
Museum of Art,
R. Lehman Collection

Compared with Van Eyck's *Giovanni Arnolfini and his bride*, this portrait of a marriage is a lifeless work in which the saint has a central place, and all the attention is actually focused on the curiosities on the table because all the light falls on them. Because of the unusual composition and sensitive treatment - for that time - of the "dead" objects, this work can be viewed as an early precursor of the genre pieces and still lifes of the seventeenth century.

Robert Campin, c. 1375-1444,
the Master of Flémalle
The Birth of Christ, c. 1420/30
Panel, 87 x 70 cm
Dijon, Musée des Beaux-Arts

The subtlety and detailed elaboration which characterizes Jan van Eyck is absent in Campin, in whose work the powerful composition and plasticity are the central features.

Hans Memling, c. 1433-1494
Portrait of an Italian with
a Roman Coin
(Giovanni de Candida), 1470
Panel, 29 x 22 cm
Antwerp, Royal Museum
of Fine Arts

With Memling, panel painting achieved its final zenith in Bruges. He was considered the best portrait painter of the Flemish primitives. His portraits are characterized by an unusual sensitivity and almost mystical atmosphere.

Rogier van der Weyden, c. 1399-1464
Mary and Child, St. Peter, John the Baptist,
Cosmas and Damianus, c. 1450
Panel, 53 x 38 cm
Frankfurt, Städelsches Kunstinstitut

Robert Campin's pupil overshadowed his master with his religious portraits. Both his paintings and his statues had an important influence on north European painting and sculpture between 1450 and 1500.

Juan de Flandes, demonstrable
between 1496-1519
The Beheading of
John the Baptist
Panel, 88 x 47 cm
Geneva, Musée d'Art
et d'Histoire

This Dutch-Spanish artist was
the painter at the court of
Isabella of Castille in Spain
from 1496. He painted a large
series of panels of the life of
Christ and Mary for her. This
work is one of these. Juan de
Flandes was a great influence
on the Dutch school of
Spanish painting.

Hugo van der Goes, c. 1440-1482, The Fall, left-hand panel of a diptych, before 1470
Panel, 33.8 x 23.2 cm, Vienna, Kunsthistorisches Museum

This representation of the Fall is dominated by an atmosphere of melancholy in which even the
"snake" - here a sort of salamander with a female face - is fearful rather than satisfied about the
successful temptation of Eve.

Joachim Patenier, c. 1480-1524
Charon crosses the River Styx to the Underworld, c. 1522
Panel, 64 x 103 cm
Madrid, The Prado

Patenier made a significant contribution to the development of landscape painting in the early sixteenth century. The landscape, which had always played a subordinate, decorative or symbolic role, acquired an importance of its own in his work. He created spatial depth, not by using perspective, but by the use of colours passing from warm to cold hues (from green-brown to green-blue), as can be clearly seen in this work.

Master of the Legend of St. Lucia, working between 1483-1501
Madonna with the Female Saints, c. 1489
Panel, 108 x 171 cm
Brussels, Royal Museum for Fine Arts

Gerard David, c. 1460-1523
Madonna with Angels and Saints, 1509
Panel, 120 x 213 cm
Rouen, Musée des Beaux-Arts

There is an interesting difference between these two Madonnas. The older panel still faithfully follows the ideal of Gothic Art; the figures are not realistic, as in David's work, but represent unearthly spirituality.

Herri met de Bles, c. 1500-1550/1560
St. John on Patmos, c. 1535/50
Panel, 33 x 47 cm
Antwerp, Royal Museum for Fine Arts

This painter, probably Patenier's nephew, followed Leonardo da Vinci's instructions on how to create depth in the landscape; objects in the distance disappear in a light mist.

Quentin Massys, c. 1464/65-1530
Portrait of a Man, c. 1520-30
Panel, 80 x 64.5 cm
Edinburgh, National Gallery of Scotland

This portrait may have been painted together with Patenier, who also painted the landscape in another portrait by Massys.

31

Jan van Hemessen, actually Jan Sanders, c. 1500-1575
The Surgeon, c, 1555
Panel, 100 x 141 cm
Madrid, The Prado

Realistic scenes from daily life with a tendency to caricature were Jan van Hemessen's
favourite subjects. The surgeon is cutting out a "stone". There was a superstitious belief that
madness was lodged in the head in the form of a stone which could be cut out. It is striking
that the characters are not wearing contemporary clothes, but fifteen century Burgundian
clothes.

Jan Gossaert, known as Mabuse, c. 1478-1532
Danaë, 1527
Panel, 113.5 x 95 cm
Munich, Alte Pinakothek

The study trip to Italy which Gossaert made in 1508 had a permanent influence on his work. He was
one of the first artists to paint historical and mythological representations with naked figures,
although the combination of Italian and Flemish styles sometimes results in an unharmonious whole.

33

Pieter Bruegel, c. 1528/30-1569, The Peasant Dance, c. 1568
Panel, 114 x 164 cm
Vienna, Kunsthistorisches Museum

Celebrating the saint's day of a patron saint, the villagers drink copiously and behave in a dissolute way. At first sight this is a joyful scene, but it is probably a moralizing work about the abhorrence of such exuberance, which the Church in those days regularly tried to suppress.

Pieter Bruegel, c. 1528/30-1569, The Return of the Hunters, 1565
Panel, 117 x 159 cm
Vienna, Kunsthistorisches Museum

This scene, which is probably one of a series of twelve representing the twelve months, is one of the most beautiful winter landscapes in European art. The month shown in this painting is probably February, and the landscape merges from the Flemish countryside to rugged mountains.

Pieter Bruegel, c. 1528/30-1569, The Tower of Babel, c. 1563
Panel, 114 x 155 cm
Vienna, Kunsthistorisches Museum

In the foreground, King Nimrod gives orders to work on his monstrous tower which reaches up to the clouds and dominates the whole area. The construction of the tower reflects Bruegel's extensive knowledge of architecture and building.

Jan Bruegel the Elder, 1568-1625, Paradise
Copper, 29 x 38 cm
Frankfurt, Städelsches Kunstinstitut

Pieter Bruegel's youngest son was known as the "Velvet Bruegel". He excelled in landscapes and flower arrangements with a subtle use of colour, as shown in this landscape from his imagination, painted on copper.

Roelant Savery, 1576-1639, Landscape with Birds, 1628
Copper, 42 x 57 cm
Vienna, Kunsthistorisches Museum

The main subject of this singular artist was a miraculous world, populated by the most diverse creatures. In this work he has depicted a bizarre kingdom of birds.

Gillis Claesz. d'Hondecoeter, c. 1575-1638, Landscape, 1613
Canvas, 49 x 83 cm
Antwerp, Royal Museum of Fine Arts

The foreground of this landscape no longer serves to create a sense of depth, but has actually become a predominant element. This interpretation of the landscape which was developed by Gillis van Coninxloo (1544-1607), was further elaborated by Hondecoeter.

Peter Paul Rubens, 1577-1640, and Jan Bruegel the Elder, 1568-1625
Madonna in a Garland of Flowers, c. 1616-18, (The garland was painted by Jan Bruegel the Elder)
Panel, 158 x 210 cm, Munich, Alte Pinakothek

In the garland of flowers the colours have a symbolic significance. It was painted by Jan
Bruegel, who painted both the flowers and landscapes in a number of works by Rubens, who
executed the human figures himself.

Jan Bruegel the Elder, 1568-1625, A Large Bouquet in a Tub, c. 1610
Panel, 124.5 x 96.2 cm
Munich, Alte Pinakothek

One of the many magnificent still lifes of flowers in which Jan Bruegel showed his mastery of the
minute detail in the wealth of forms and colours.

Abraham Janssens, before 1575-1632, Olympus, c. 1615
Canvas, 207 x 240 cm
Munich, Alte Pinakothek

Janssens was considered to be one of the last Romanists - painters who went to Italy and then
worked entirely under the Italian influence. In his "Olympus", a very popular subject at that time, the
figures are extremely close to the observer, which creates an overwhelming effect in this composition.
It is rather unbalanced because of the different stylistic elements which Janssens incorporated in it.

Peter Paul Rubens, 1577-1640, Rubens and Isabella Brant in the Bower of Honeysuckle, c. 1609
Canvas, 178 x 136 cm
Munich, Alte Pinakothek

This elegant and tender portrait shows the painter as a patrician with his eighteen-year-old bride. It is
unusual that both are portrayed as full-length figures, because in those days this was customary only
for royalty and the nobility.

Peter Paul Rubens, 1577-1640, Castor and Pollux Abduct the Daughters of Leukyppos
Canvas, 222 x 209 cm
Munich, Alte Pinakothek

The way in which Rubens painted the human skin is particularly striking in this work, in which the white bodies of the women contrast with the tanned skin of the men and the brown horse.

Peter Paul Rubens, 1577-1640
The Battle of the Amazons, c. 1618/20
Panel, 121 x 165.5 cm
Munich, Bayerische Staatsgemäldesammlungen

The battle on the bridge is based on Leonardo da Vinci's "Battle of Anghiari". This work has been lost, and we know it mainly through copies by Rubens. The panel also contains references to ancient sarcophagi which often depicted this battle.

Peter Paul Rubens, 1577-1640
The Fur Cloak, 1636-39
Panel, 176 x 83 cm
Vienna, Kunsthistorisches Museum

After Isabella's death in 1624,
Rubens remarried the
sixteen-year-old Hélène Fourment
four years later. He painted this
intimate portrait of her for himself,
and left it to her in his will so that it
would stay in the family.

Peter Paul Rubens, 1577-1640, Madonna with the Saints, c. 1638-40
Panel, 211 x 195 cm
Antwerp, Sint Jacobskerk

This late painting, which Rubens made for himself, and which he wished to have over his tomb, is one of his most striking religious works.

Anthony van Dyck, 1599-1641
Portrait of a Distinguished Lady
with her Daughter, c. 1627/32
Canvas, 204 x 135 cm
Paris, The Louvre

Van Dyck painted portraits
virtually only of aristocrats and
prosperous burghers, such as
this elegant lady with her rather
shy daughter looking on. The
artist has perfectly captured the
facial expression which almost
suggests that she has been
caught unawares.

Anthony van Dyck, 1599-1641, Charles I on Horseback
c. 1635/40, canvas, 123 x 85 cm
Madrid, The Prado

The great portrait painter, Van Dyck, who was a pupil and an assistant of Rubens from 1617 to 1621,
became the court painter of the English king, Charles I, shown here, in 1630, after being appointed
the court painter of the Archduchess Isabella in 1627.

Jacob I Jordaens, 1593-1678
Ferry Boat to Antwerp, c. 1623
Canvas, 281 x 468 cm
Copenhagen, Statens Museum for Kunst

Apart from Rubens and Van Dyck, Jordaens was the most important seventeenth century
Flemish painter. Although he never travelled to Italy, the influence of painters such as
Caravaggio is clearly present in his work. The second major influence was Rubens, for whom
he also worked several times on large commissions. Mythological, biblical and allegorical
themes form the most important subjects in his oeuvre.

Jacob I Jordaens, 1593-1678
Pan and Syrinx, c. 1625
Canvas, 173 x 136 cm
Brussels, Royal Museum for Fine Arts

49

David Teniers de Jonge, 1610-1690, The Art Collection of Archduke Leopold-Willem in Brussels, 1651
Canvas, 127 x 162.5 cm
Sussex, Petworth House, The National Trust

This successful painter specialized in genre pieces and portraits, and his total oeuvre comprises almost 2,000 works. He is shown here with the Archduke in the gallery; he was employed as court painter. It is a characteristic work in terms of the style and taste of artists and collectors during the baroque period who liked to be portrayed as art lovers.

Frans Snijders, 1579-1657, Flowers, Fruit and Vegetables
Canvas, 165 x 233 cm
Antwerp, Royal Museum for Fine Arts

Snijders is the most important painter of Flemish still lifes in the monumental style of Rubens. He was the first to paint still lifes of game and birds. His compositions are often animated by the presence of living creatures, such as the monkey and the little dog in this work.

Cornelis de Vos, 1584-1651
Portrait of the Artist with
his Family, 1621
Canvas, 188 x 162 cm
Brussels, Royal Museum for
Fine Arts

The portrait painter, De Vos,
was particularly famous for the
expressive eyes of his figures.
The nuances in the ways in
which the members of the
family are looking are a
splendid illustration of this.

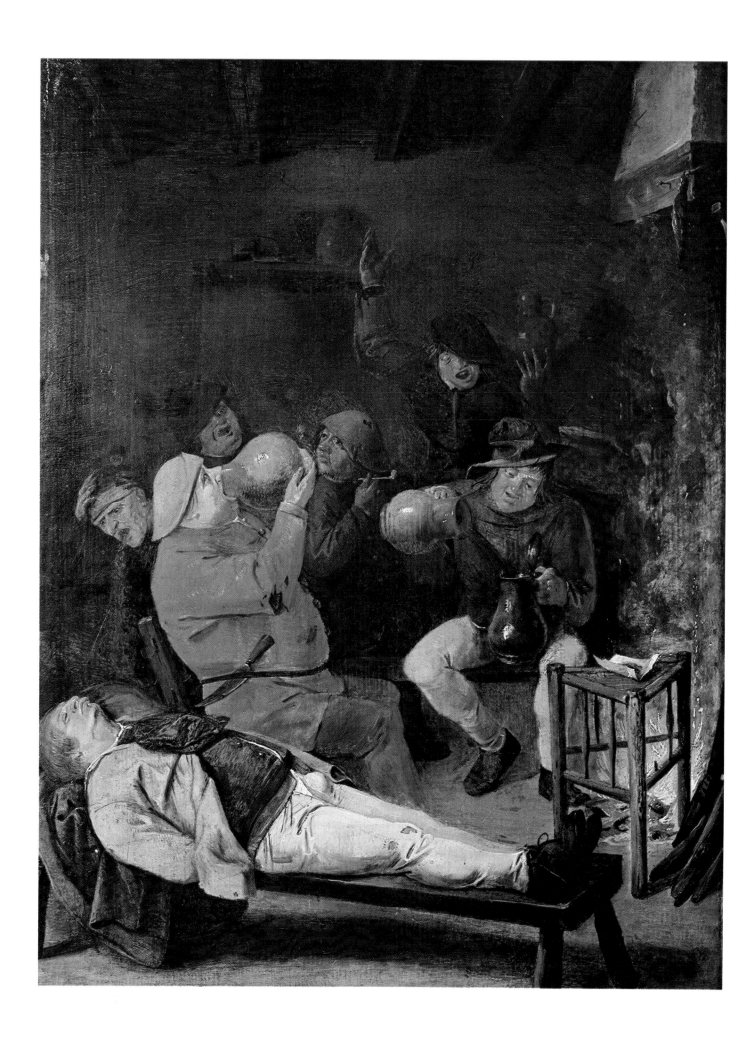

Adriaen Brouwer,
c. 1605/06-1638
Portrait of a Man with
a Pointed Hat
Panel, 19.5 x 12 cm
Rotterdam, Boymans -
van Beuningen Museum

Brouwer, who died at a very young age, combined the subjects of Pieter Bruegel and the stylistic influences of Frans Hals and Rubens, in a surprising and lively way. He specialized in scenes in inns, and festivities. This "Scene at the Inn" is a good example of this. Rubens and Rembrandt collected the work of this painter, who also painted a number of extremely important works as a portraitist and landscape painter.

Adriaen Brouwer, c. 1605/06-1638
Scene at the Inn, c. 1624-25
Panel, 34.8 x 26 cm
Rotterdam, Boymans - van Beuningen Museum

Osias Beert, 1570-1624 (?), Oysters and Glasses
Panel, 43 x 54 cm, Madrid, Prado Museum

A so-called "breakfast" by this master of still lifes, of whom only eight works are known.

Ambrosius II Bosschaert, 1573-1621, Flowers on a Windowsill, c. 1619-20
Panel, 64 x 46 cm, The Hague, Mauritshuis

This great representative of the seventeenth-century Dutch still life was one of the first painters who concentrated entirely on still lifes with bouquets of flowers and fruit.

Page 56: Daniel Seghers, 1590-1661, St. Goswin surrounded by Flowers
Canvas, 95 x 68 cm, Rome, Pinakotheca Vaticana

This pupil of the "Velvet Bruegel" was well known as a painter of flowers. He specialized in painting garlands of flowers to frame religious scenes.